THE LITTLE BOOK OF

big ideas

ABOUT

Hope

elaine cannon

EAGLE
GATE

Library of Congress Catalog Card Number 00-133331

ISBN 1-57345-827-9

Printed in Mexico   18961-6722

10   9   8   7   6   5   4   3   2   1

is the eighth letter in the alphabet
and, like baptism at age eight, it is
the beginning of

Hope.

Hope springs from remembering Heavenly Father's tender mercies.

With our smallest recognition of God's goodness, of his *being* there for us—even in seemingly small experiences—we want to sing, shout, clap, laugh, weep, and surely fall upon our knees in gratitude.

Hope takes us to a higher plane of thought and is spiritually encompassing. It prepares us to take heart when our need is great. It leads us to *expect* him to provide guidance, balance, understanding, comfort. There is no other complete source of

solace, satisfaction, peace, and surety than
Jesus Christ. Jesus is the source of Hope. And
with all we have, he has yet more in store for us.
Said Sister Mary Corita, "To believe in God is
to know all the rules will be fair and there will
be wonderful surprises." May you find delight in
this little book of big ideas about hope. May
hope become your "shadow by day and your
pillar by night."

Elaine Cannon

Roget's Thesaurus of English words and phrases is
a good place to start in defining the word hope—
for both its usage and the glorious feeling it stirs.
Hope is expectation, belief, certainty, probability,
buoyancy, cheerfulness, assurance, confidence,
faith, possibility, a break in the clouds, and clear
comfort about going forward.

WORLDLY HOPE IS WISHFUL THINKING, GENTLE

DREAMING OF FAIRIES, MAGIC WANDS, AND

LIMITLESS CREDIT CARD BALANCES. CHRIST-

CENTERED HOPE FOCUSES ON THE TRUTH

THAT WITH GOD NOTHING IS IMPOSSIBLE.

The sacred phrase

of Christmas,

"fear not,"

empowers hope

(LUKE 2:10).

o hope is to rest assured, to feel confident, to rely or lean on. But in the highest sense, hope is often linked with God's help, particularly if what we are hoping for is something wholesome but difficult to attain.

Emily Dickinson, nineteenth century
romantic poet, described hope this way:

Hope is the thing with feathers
That perches in the soul,
And sings the tunes without the words,
And never stops at all.

A SCRIPTURE TO MOUNT ON YOUR

MEMO BOARD IS FROM PAUL TO THE

ROMANS: "THE SPIRIT ITSELF BEARETH

WITNESS WITH OUR SPIRIT, THAT WE ARE

THE CHILDREN OF GOD" (ROMANS 8:16).

WHAT A LOVELY THING TO KNOW!

Personally, I feel charged with the clarion call offered by President Hugh B. Brown: "Then let us prepare for the future unafraid. Let faith replace fear. Let courage dispel gloom. Let hope triumph over despair, and let faith in God the Eternal Father reign supreme above all our works."

Face it, life is not about perfection
and fulfillment; it is about hanging
in there, hopefully sloshing through
trials toward personal growth.

THE FOREVER THEME OF THINGS FOCUSES

ON CHRIST AND HIS ATONEMENT—HIS GIFT

TO US OF DEATH CONQUERED, OF HOPE IN

ETERNAL LIFE WITH SATISFYING HAPPINESS.

Never forget
the slogan, "not
that we *can* hope,
but that we *must*!"

A frightening thread of truth about a large percentage of mankind are these words written by Mormon, the Lamanite hero: *"But behold, I was without hope, for I knew the judgments of the Lord which should come upon them; for they repented not of their iniquities, but did struggle for their lives without calling upon that Being who created them"* (MORMON 5:2).

SOMEONE GAVE ME A CHARMING ACCESSORY,

OFFERING A REASSURING LIFT IN DIFFICULT TIMES.

IT IS STAINED GLASS WITH THE WORDS: JE T'AIME

PLUS QU'HIER, MOINS QUE DEMAIN. (I LOVE YOU

MORE THAN YESTERDAY, LESS THAN TOMORROW.)

Elder Neal A. Maxwell gave a message of encouragement to faithful people who languish in hospitals and nursing homes: "Take courage; revive your spirits and strengthen your faith. In these lessons so impressively taught in precept and example by our great exemplar, Jesus Christ, and his Prophet of the restoration, Joseph Smith, we have ample inspiration for comfort and for hope."

Often while reading the works of gifted
thinkers, a ray of hope lightens the mind.
Do you recall Felicia's lines in act three
of Jean Kerr's play *Finishing Touches*?
"Hope is the feeling you have that the
feeling you have isn't permanent."

Claudio, in Shakespeare's *Measure for Measure*, opines, "The miserable have no other medicine but only hope." While Václav Havel, author and president of the Czech Republic, refined the definition: "Hope is definitely not the same thing as optimism. It is not the conviction that something will turn out well, but the certainty that something makes sense, regardless of how it turns out."

IN 1750, SAMUEL JOHNSON SAID

SOMETHING THAT IS STILL SUITABLE

TODAY: "THE NATURAL FLIGHTS OF

THE HUMAN MIND ARE NOT FROM

PLEASURE TO PLEASURE, BUT FROM

HOPE TO HOPE."

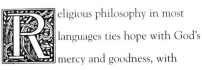eligious philosophy in most languages ties hope with God's mercy and goodness, with man's ability and choice of behavior to wax confident before a God who is trusted. The person who is a disciple of Christ, currently suffering an ordeal, finds that hope gives trials meaning and the promise of vanishing altogether.

It is well for a seeker after peace to receive the blessing of the Comforter, who fills us with hope and blessed contentment. Without this spirit, one cannot feel elation in relief.

Stephen L Richards spoke at the funeral of a relative. He emphasized that not only is the family a basic unit for happy life and progress here on this earth, but that it also constitutes the very foundation of our hope for supreme exaltation in the celestial kingdom of our God.

LEVI EDGAR YOUNG spoke of missionaries, but it seems to apply as well to all of us striving through life: "No sooner has the faith and the hope of an illuminated future taken hold of him than he is desirous to disseminate this possession to all the world."

To anyone aching for a feeling of hope in eternal life, Melvin J. Ballard advised this remembrance: "O, how wonderful are the provisions of our Father to meet all the emergencies of life—its joys, its sorrows, its distresses. Here is a gospel that meets all emergencies."

resident Joseph F. Smith said: "We pray God to bless and comfort those who are bereaved more especially by their loss; and their hearts may not faint, but that they may be buoyed up in the hope of the glorious resurrection awaiting them when they and their loved ones shall be reunited in the life and light which will never perish or again grow dim."

PEOPLE WHO HAVE STUDIED THE TEACHINGS OF JESUS
WILL ADMIT TO THE PERSPECTIVE OF HOPE FOUND IN THE
ACCOUNT OF THE APOSTLES OF OLD WHEN THE SAVIOR
ASKED THEM, AFTER A NUMBER HAD FORSAKEN HIM,
"WILL YE ALSO FORSAKE ME?" THEIR ANSWER ECHOES
OURS, "WHERE CAN WE GO TO FIND PEACE, AND COM-
FORT, AND HOPE, IF WE TURN AWAY FROM TRUTH?"

THREE VITAL TRUTHS ABOUT HOPE WERE SAID
BY JESUS: (1) "IF YE SHALL ASK ANY THING IN
MY NAME, I WILL DO IT"; (2) "IF YE LOVE ME,
KEEP MY COMMANDMENTS"; (3) "I WILL NOT
LEAVE YOU COMFORTLESS" (JOHN 14:14–15, 18).

If we seek the joyful lift of hope, let us not be
swayed by the skeptics of the world who ignore
or reject truth. There is no meaning and no hope
in all we do if we deny the truth of Christ as
our necessary Redeemer and generous friend.

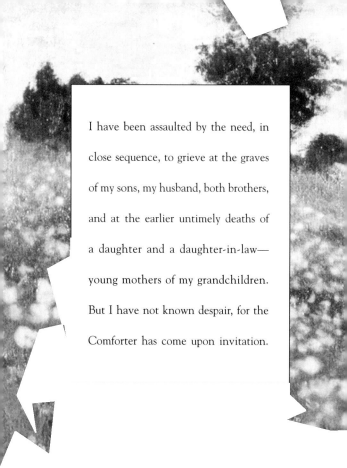

I have been assaulted by the need, in close sequence, to grieve at the graves of my sons, my husband, both brothers, and at the earlier untimely deaths of a daughter and a daughter-in-law— young mothers of my grandchildren. But I have not known despair, for the Comforter has come upon invitation.

WE ARE A FOOLISH GENERATION TO QUIBBLE
ABOUT THE VIEWS OF LIFE AND DEATH WITH
PEOPLE WHO HAVE NOT LEARNED THE MATTER
OF GOD'S PLAN. THERE IS HOPE IN OUR
CREATOR'S PLAN OF HAPPINESS FOR US WITH
THE PROMISE THAT THE SAME SOCIALITY WE
ENJOY IN THIS LIFE WE CAN ENJOY IN THE
NEXT—ONLY IT WILL BE MORE MARVELOUS!

(D&C 130:2)

Think back on ancient history and see that God has never left his children without hope. With an oath and covenant, God gave old Father Abraham and all his posterity (that's us!) the hope of life eternal and, for those faithful and true, *exaltation!*

THE GREATEST TRUTH KNOWN TO MAN IS

THAT THERE REALLY IS A GOD IN HEAVEN

IN CHARGE OF THE UNIVERSE—AND ALL

PEOPLE HE CREATED—AND WHO IS THE

PRESERVER OF THE PLAN AND PROMISES.

THERE IS NOTHING TO FEAR, REALLY. YOU HAVE
HOPE IN CHRIST. THEN PAY ATTENTION TO
YOUR PERSPECTIVE ABOUT SUCH SHATTERING
TRIALS AS BEING SINGLE, BANKRUPT, REJECTED,
TERMINALLY ILL, UNHAPPY IN A RELATIONSHIP.
LIKE THE HYMN SAYS, "GIRD UP YOUR LOINS,
FRESH COURAGE TAKE" TO FACE THE DAY.

Representatives from the families of each of my parents' children finished closing the cabin so dear for twenty-five years. It had been sold. Packed up along with cast-iron kettles, tattered books, worn life jackets, and ancient fishing gear were memories so precious we wept as we boxed them for Deseret Industries. But the warmth and love moved with us. It flourishes still whenever we gather again, in whatever place, until we meet beyond the veil.

It doesn't matter how tall

or small we are, it is what we

are inside, where hope springs,

that counts forever.

How can anyone feel depressed,
lonely, or without hope in the midst
of life's incredible blessings, as well
as a world full of natural wonders
and interesting human beings?
With a soaring soul, thank God!

gency is an

absolute in the eternal scheme of things; so

peace, love, faith, and hope come when you

ask God for them and then work for them

as if everything depends upon you.

It is hope that maintains most of mankind,

according to Samuel Johnson, because when

there is no hope, there can be no endeavor.

Things past belong

to memory alone;

things future are the

property of hope.

Dante's *Inferno* carries the phrase of

fear, which is the opposite of hope:

"Abandon hope, all ye who enter

here [purgatory]."

For anyone assaulted with hard times and

blue memories, comfort can come by turning

to the word of God.

For example: "Wherefore, whoso believeth in God might with surety hope for a better world, yea, even a place at the right hand of God, which hope cometh of faith, maketh an anchor to the souls of men, which would make them sure and steadfast, always abounding in good works, being led to glorify God" (ETHER 12:4).

A haunting bit of advice from Ira Gershwin: "Never let the clouds cover the sun for long."

olly Heather
learned valuable lessons through hardship
and thus wrote: "As I continue to believe
and to keep the Lord's commandments, the
little light inside me grows just a bit brighter.
The peace that comes from hope is making
me ever more sure and steadfast."

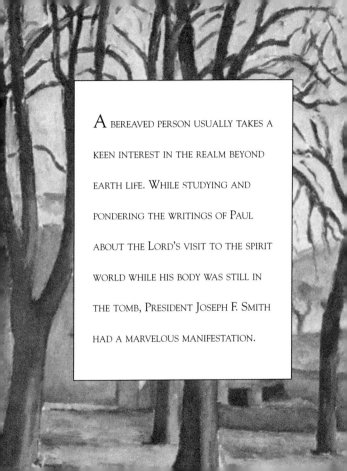

A BEREAVED PERSON USUALLY TAKES A KEEN INTEREST IN THE REALM BEYOND EARTH LIFE. WHILE STUDYING AND PONDERING THE WRITINGS OF PAUL ABOUT THE LORD'S VISIT TO THE SPIRIT WORLD WHILE HIS BODY WAS STILL IN THE TOMB, PRESIDENT JOSEPH F. SMITH HAD A MARVELOUS MANIFESTATION.

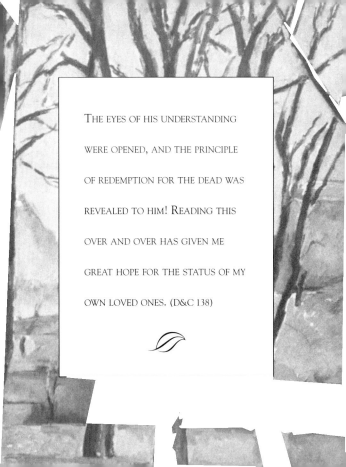

THE EYES OF HIS UNDERSTANDING WERE OPENED, AND THE PRINCIPLE OF REDEMPTION FOR THE DEAD WAS REVEALED TO HIM! READING THIS OVER AND OVER HAS GIVEN ME GREAT HOPE FOR THE STATUS OF MY OWN LOVED ONES. (D&C 138)

"We stand, and rejoice in hope of the glory of God. And not only so, but we glory in tribulations also: knowing that tribulation worketh patience; and patience, experience; and experience, hope: and hope maketh not ashamed; because the love of God is shed abroad in our hearts by the Holy Ghost which is given unto us" (ROMANS 5:2–5).

Personal progress is changing for the better, which means drawing closer to God in some way. We simply cannot be happy apart from the Savior. Life is so designed by him.

BEHIND OUR CONSTANT EFFORT TO COPE

WITH DISAPPOINTMENT AND IMPERFECTION

IS THE TRUTH THAT GOD LOVES EACH OF

US, HIS CHILDREN. THE SPARK OF THE DIVINE

IS IN EACH OF US! OUR HOPE IS IN HIM WHO

IS THE MODEL FOR OUR LIVES. THERE IS

BEAUTY AND HOPE IN THE ASSURANCE

SHARED BY PRESIDENT DAVID O. MCKAY:

"As absolute as the certainty that you have in your hearts that tonight will be followed by dawn tomorrow morning, so is my assurance that Jesus Christ is the Savior of mankind, the light that will dispel the darkness of the world, through the gospel restored by direct revelation to the Prophet Joseph Smith."

The basis of hope is that with

all we have and all we know,

He holds yet more.

I know that as we approach Heavenly Father in the name of Jesus Christ, he will draw close to us. Our hearts and minds will be ready to receive his tutoring. Hope is the fuel through which the ideal becomes real; and with God's help, the ideal *can* become real with hope as the fuel.

I TENDERLY THANK HEAVENLY FATHER FOR EVERY CARING TEACHER WHO HAS TAUGHT ME THE GOSPEL OF HOPE IN JESUS CHRIST. THEY HAVE HELPED PREPARE ME FOR THE WRENCHING MOMENTS OF LIFE. HOW DO PEOPLE ENDURE HOLLOW HEART TIMES WITHOUT THE HOPE THAT TRAINING AND EXPERIENCE HAVE GIVEN ME?

"How do you do it?" a woman asked me after a close series of family heartaches. I replied flippantly with a wry smile, "One dreadful day after another!" Then I explained in serious gratitude that the hope of reunion is real when you draw close enough to Christ for a good view.

The mature, troubled priesthood
leader had been worn weary and
weakened. He had fallen short of his
covenants; paid the terrible price of
guilt and shame (they are not exactly
the same, you know); suffered sorrow,
panic, worry, stress; and for a time
indulged in useless rationalization,
cowardice, and depression. When, at

last, his blessings were restored and he left the office of the proper priesthood person, he saw an apostle of the Lord, to whom he was not personally known, cross in front of him. "It was a sign," the joyous friend said. "Say what you want, but I know the timing was God's tangible gift to me. Through it all, He had been my hope! It was incredible to find myself flooded with the Holy Ghost again, and I stood in that public place weeping like a child."

have hope in the dear Lord. Likely I will have no control over whatever memorial service ushers me through death's veil into heaven, so I now include my personal creed as a "bowing out" prayer. These lines that say it for me are from the pen of St. Francis of Assisi. (They were written centuries before my time, but truth is always relevant, and humans in God's name have no time slot, do they?) I intend to find *him* up there as well!

Lord, make me an instrument of thy peace.

Where there is hatred, let me sow love;

Where there is doubt, let me sow faith;

Where there is despair, let me sow hope;

Where there is darkness, let me sow light;

Where there is sadness, let me sow joy!

O divine Master, Grant that I may not so much seek

To be consoled as to console,

To be understood as to understand,

To be loved as to love.

For it is in giving that we receive;

It is in pardoning that we are pardoned,

And it is in dying that we are born to eternal life.

When David, a psalmist as well as a King,
sorrowed for his sins, eloquent phrasing
and tender expression became a legacy for
our own hope. He wrote: "For mine
iniquities . . . are too heavy for me. . . .
I am troubled; I am bowed down greatly;
I go mourning all the day long. . . . For in
thee, O Lord, do I hope" (PSALM 38:4–15).

Our hope in Jesus is that he is more than a great teacher, as some in the world explain him. I know that Jesus *is* what he himself said he was—the Son of God, the Only Begotten in the flesh, our Savior and necessary Redeemer, the Christ. He is waiting to be gracious to us again and again, as long as it takes.

There is *Hope!*

about the author

Elaine Cannon continues to bring impressive experience, insight, and delight in her writing. In her long career, Mrs. Cannon has authored more than fifty books and has received numerous honors and awards for her work.

ISBN 1-57345-827-9

50795

9 781573 458276

SKU 4024462 U.S. $7.95